CRANES

by Lisa Bullard

Lerner Publications Company • Minneapolis

Special thanks to Tony Phillippi of Phillippi Equipment Company, for sharing his enthusiasm and for letting me visit the wonderful cranes in his "sandbox."

This book is dedicated to Max, who always does such a great job of lifting me up.

Text copyright © 2007 by Lisa Bullard

Lerner Publications Company
A division of Lerner Publishing Group
41 First Avenue North
Minneapolis, MN 55401 U.S.A.

Website address: www.lernerbooks.com

Words in **bold type** are explained in a glossary on page 30.

Library of Congress Cataloging-in-Publication Data

Bullard, Lisa.
    Cranes / by Lisa Bullard.
      p.   cm. — (Pull ahead books)
    Includes index.
    ISBN-13: 978-0-8225-6007-4 (lib. bdg. : alk. paper)
    ISBN-10: 0-8225-6007-0 (lib. bdg. : alk. paper)
    1. Cranes, derricks, etc.—Juvenile literature. I. Title. II.
Series.
TJ1363.B924 2007
621.8'73—dc22   2005020651

Manufactured in the United States of America
1 2 3 4 5 6 – JR – 12 11 10 09 08 07

What is this tall machine?

It's a crane! Cranes lift heavy loads up high.

Cranes can also move things from one place to another. This crane is moving a giant pipe.

Builders use cranes. They need them when they build something big.

These cranes are helping to build a new bridge.

Cranes can do jobs other than building. This crane loads train cars.

These cranes move big boxes on and off ships.

This crane is carrying a wrecking ball.
Wham! The wrecking ball is knocking
down an old building.

Some cranes are built for special jobs.
This crane lifts and carries the space
shuttle.

Cranes
can even
help people
change
lightbulbs!

Different cranes do different jobs.
These tower cranes help build
a building.

Tower cranes are some of the biggest cranes in the world. They can be as tall as a skyscraper.

The tall part of a tower crane is called the tower, or **mast.**

Builders add extra pieces to make the tower taller. The tower grows as the building grows.

The tower has two arms. The long arm is the **main jib.** The main jib carries the loads.

The short arm is sometimes called the **counter-jib.**

The blocks on the counter-jib are called **counterweights.** They keep the crane from tipping when it lifts something.

The **slewing gear** turns the jibs. Then they point in a different direction.

The cab sits on top of the slewing gear.
Who is that inside?

The **operator** sits in the cab. The
operator uses many controls to work
the crane. See how high up the
operator is?

The operator moves the **trolley** back and forth along the main jib.

A hook hangs from the trolley. The operator can make the hook go up or down.

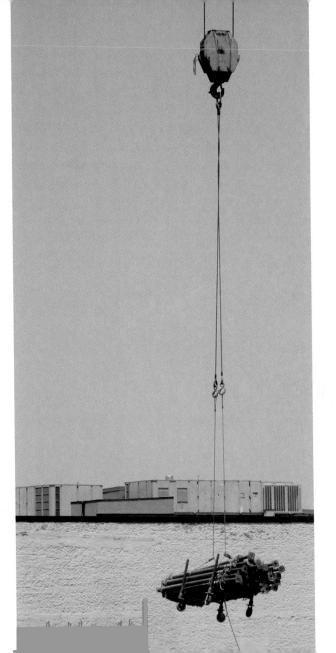

The hook is lifting a heavy load of building supplies.

Finally, the building is almost finished!
What will happen to the tower crane?

Builders will take the crane apart and move it. Soon the crane will have another important job to do!

Facts about Cranes

■ Sometimes skyscrapers are built with a tower crane inside of them. The crane sits inside a hole in the building. Workers take out the crane in pieces when the skyscraper is finished. The hole that is left is turned into an elevator shaft.

■ Cranes have helped to build many important things. The Empire State Building in New York City, the Gateway Arch in St. Louis, Hoover Dam in the southwestern United States, and the tallest skyscrapers in the world were all built using cranes. Cranes have even been used to build things in outer space!

■ Cranes are able to lift heavy loads by using pulleys. Pulleys are simple machines that include a system of wheels and ropes.

Parts of a Tower Crane

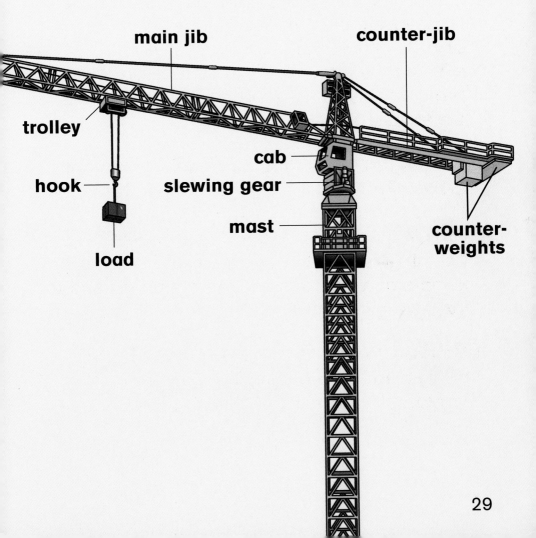

main jib

counter-jib

trolley

cab

slewing gear

hook

mast

load

counter-weights

Glossary

counter-jib: the shorter arm of a tower crane. It is also called the machinery arm.

counterweights: heavy pieces that look like big blocks. They keep the crane in balance when it lifts a large load.

main jib: the longer arm of a tower crane. It carries the load.

mast: the tall part of a tower crane that stands straight up. It is also called the tower.

operator: the person who runs the crane

slewing gear: the part of a tower crane that turns the jibs

trolley: a part that runs back and forth along a tower crane's main jib

More about Cranes

Check out these books and this website to find out more about cranes.

Books

Korman, Justine H. *Building the Skyscraper.* New York: Scholastic, 1999.
Watch cranes at work in this fun illustrated book about building skyscrapers.

Randolph, Joanne. *Cranes.* New York: PowerKids Press, 2002.
Learn more from this book about cranes and how they work.

Rogers, Hal. *Cranes.* Chanhassen, MN: Child's World, 1999.
This book has many pictures of cranes in action.

Website

Kikki's Workshop
http://www.kenkenkikki.jp/e_index2.html
This website has videos that show how cranes and other construction equipment work. The site also has pictures and games and lots of other fun stuff for kids.

Index

builders, 6, 16, 27

cab, 21, 22

counter-jib, 18, 19

counterweights, 19

hook, 24, 25

main jib, 17, 23

mast, 15

operator, 22, 23, 24

slewing gear, 20, 21

tower crane, 13, 14, 15, 26

trolley, 23, 24

Photo Acknowledgments

© Todd Strand/Independent Picture Service, front cover, pp. 13, 14, 15, 17, 18, 19, 20, 21, 23, 24, 25, ; © David Lane/Palm Beach Post/ZUMA Press, p. 3; © Royalty-Free/ CORBIS, pp. 4, 5, 12, 16, 22; © Owen Franken/CORBIS, p. 6; © Sacramento Bee/Michael A. Jones/ZUMA Press, p. 7; © Dick Loek/ZUMA Press, p. 8; © Gunter Marx Photography/CORBIS, p. 9; © SuperStock, Inc./ SuperStock, p. 10; NASA, p. 11; © Alan Schein Photography/CORBIS, p. 26; © AP|Wide World Photos, p. 27. Illustration on p. 29 by Laura Westlund.